MW00976936

Where the Dust Collects

by

Lottie Larsa

WHERE THE DUST COLLECTS

First edition published 2021.
Second edition 2023.

ISBN: 978-1-7379797-6-0 (paperback)
ISBN: 978-1-7379797-7-7 (hardback)
ISBN: 978-1-7379797-8-4 (ebook)

(..)

For no one

(hehehe)

Contents

~

my happiness stolen
but my mind unconcerned
till I woke up to find
my madness returned

~

In the Soundless Denouement

At the end of things
There is comfort in the knowing

A ram's head assuredness
That pillows the murmured
Collateral

Falling turrets by the lakeside
Where it drinks with legs spread
Wining down its neck curve
In staggered, exposing necessity

Thirsting inertia
To the striking from behind

Killing it
As in want of air

      Such is the disquiet of my mind

Covetous to know direction
The point
Where from the malady came

The owner of the mouth
That forced a heart to bleed
And keep bleeding

Till bone assimilated skin
Leaving only brain for scavenge

Brain

Unaltered
And cognizant

In matters of decay

Wetting another's lining
Asking, endless

How it came to be

Succumbing

I feel them encroaching like an oil tide.
Vine sent as serpent called
To drown or to bind
I cannot decide.

Oh
Leave me to my sleep
Not this black alarm.

Welling in pools, the squid protrudes
Beaked in salt and citrus arming —
A bed-wet suction I cannot rise from
Dragging at my tombing waist
Down
Down
Into the growling drool.

Let the mouth reek.
Let the hair knot.
You can let them be today.

You are alone.
No one will know.
You can let them be today.

Their heft upon my chest
My neck
To lose me in the undertow
Roll me in the mud once more

And further in the pot I go.

But keep that chin up
Just enough
To poke it through the tension

Give yourself that hole, that light
That singing in the surf
To feed the air in lung collapse
Beneath what they can see —

You need to keep that chin up
Just enough
Else you slip too far
Below
And someone knows you're gone.

Wax Worker

I had always been able to wait through life thankfully.
Filling cups and making myself scarce
Was the only way I knew to please people
And, if I was lucky, they would leave quickly
Not giving a passing thought to our interaction
Beyond a momentary sigh or giggle at
My sad attempts at humor.

I fear it will be different now.
I fear I have said too much.
I have overstepped pleasantries and
Can no longer expect disinterest.
I have become too much of a novelty
To be overlooked as before

And I regret it most profoundly.

Many a thirsty stranger now empties their glass
To warm it with their ear and call it compassion.
Needless to say, I have grown to resent them.
Living leeches
Every one
Plumping their bellies from my lifetime of service
With a patronage that pays in
Counterfeited empathy.

And worse still
They do not leave.

I know they do not stay out of concern for me.
I know they stay out of concern for their boredom.
But I must keep serving them.
I have no choice.
I am too poor to stop.

Ask Me Nicely

Mean your question, but ask it nicely.
You haven't hurt me yet, which is precisely
The reason I'm waiting for you now
To look up from the ground and press me as to how
You could ever have once lived without me
When just seeing my face puts you on your knee
And gives reason for all the emptiness you feel
When you're fully bereft of me. I'll let you steal
My autonomy, this time, forever
And swear on our bond that I will endeavor
To make ours a love devoid of all foolery
When my hand and my heart are connected by jewelry
Whose clarity explains the glow where we bask
And reassures you that you only had to ask
Me one question. So, make your stand
Before this fire in my chest is fanned
And passion consumes me all too completely
In my enduring refusal to love you discreetly.

The Riot Parlor

Hunger pangs adorn the walls in a
Room abuzz with the hum of needles

Such orange and splendorous intimidation —
How I shrink in the beauty of the painted.

Collaging upon their peopled sheaths
A skull, a rose, a snail…
What best proves they can intrigue.

A lyrical stippling to offset the edge
Ankle socked or fully suited
Depends on the damage of the player —

Swooning in the bath's heat
All soap shine and polish
Look down and see what you created.

A walk of coals and whiskey
Etchings of self and interest found
Ask
What foreign confidence is this?

Presenting arms
With daggers to names
These thoughts set in your permanence.
How can you be so sure of yourself?

To eat the ink and feel complete —

To sting
The proof of faith born
With or without,
Can it ever be purchased?

Bits of clot run their wild trails
To the plastic sheet
Of your bed floor.

When next your collar cracks
And they husk your muslin back
They will have the map
To join the flaps together,

Closing you in,
Pushing patterns through pinup girls
So that even the smocks will know who you are
When they file you away
And leave for the night.

But what of the neighboring slab?
The canvas unused.

No print for the pieces.
Just a screen for projection.

Their threading seals the same
Inviting a guesswork
Through some freckled constellation —

A record of change
Equal to sought vibrancy

For what could counter such attracting
Than their purposed mystery?

Downing Reach

I take heart in not knowing

Truth, however edifying.
Rigid eternity
Is somehow stricken of madness —
Edging towards heaven in narrow graves

That entrap routinely,
        Rudely —
Imploding between laughing yawns

Without reflection or notice,
Giving warred imminence to His mouthless, eating

Ire. That helpless impulse nauseates
Knowing timely horror,
Exacting roach eruption in scuttered

Sweepings over membraned earth —
Tender hatchlings in necrosis, grinding

Teeth enamel raw.
        Recumbent,
I bereave life entirely —

Withholding, in truth, how I neglected my end.

Carukia

Pulsing blooms of delicate lace,
In elegant cruelty, the plush of your face
Left me to writhe at the water's edge
As debris agonized and unfit to dredge.

I keep myself reeling in the wake of your smile,
Your savagery hidden beneath God-given style,
Flattered to faulting your shallowness in love
When you haven't a heart or a mind to speak of.

Merely the burn of being touched by your reach
Has soured my body to the bathers on the beach,
Giving rise to the spasms that leave them convinced
I'm not cleansed of you till I'm hot urine rinsed.

The prickling of hairs gives way to the throbbing
As you drift away through waters in toss —
Lacking a conscience regretful of sobbing
In the most exquisite, jealous sea I've ever come across.

Progression

I could lose it all in the pursuit of steel
And be rewarded
As millions are
With flickers of glossy finish
In sleekness and toil
If only I could want the right thing

Forget the film encasing my ears
As I slip below the surface
With galaxy thought
And waiting life

Eel in each appendage
Dipping through the current
In that chill of immediacy —
Coating force
Reminding me this is not air
This is not nothing
Move or be moved

Earth but not earth
Hugging me tightly
As I slide closer to the center pull
Rounded peg
Finding a home
In a peace that cannot stay

Through my emergence to the gravel bank
Existence mourns from me
Deepening the grays beneath my joints

Guppy-crawl as long as I can stand
Till I can no more ignore the twinge beginning

The crackle in each turn I take

The cogged stacking of my spine
As I posture straight
And set my neck

The head is cranked
The knees are clicked
The ore correct
I give in quick

I am at once
A shiny thing
And face the world
Defective

Musings of a Frenchman I

what are you
but the naked model
in a studio full of artists

too
ashamed

to draw their own bodies

Blossom Girl

Blossomed, you said.
I had blossomed, you said.
     Hands never held redder rose before.

With too fine of petals
And too sharp of nettles,
     You picked at me till my stem tore.

So I made myself ugly,
Hoping you wouldn't touch me
     And I'd finally get up off your floor —

How foolish I'd grown,
For I should have known
     That you would have liked ugly things more.

Delusion

There is a quietness in delusion
That makes for better minds.

A restful ease.
A color drain.
The ability to provoke and fascinate.

It rumbles beneath like
A Spanish bull
Foaming between the sinews

A gnarling throb of brown, bound muscle
Precarious in its waiting

The well-meaning prod
Of a stick
Or fingertip

Set as the flint point
To ignite its expanse

At the breaking of my caging seal.

For it became mine.
Mine to entertain.
Mine to distress… and yet

I fear
A madness that will define me
Beyond what I am capable
Of upholding.

The quick unthreading of hems
Growing too long to be human
Tossing the cavern of my body

Split and
Stripped to the crowd

Revealing
The ugly jigsaw of my person
Whose flesh-freed scraps were made for famish
To upset the masses in revolt.

I feel the paint start to chip
And I reach for the tape,
For the glue,
For the tack that will hold me together.

Keep me average.
Contained.
Without.

But to think,

To let the pieces fall where they may
And clatter about the floor.

To leave the body bare
Trace where the seams run
And feel them fray apart.

Wouldn't that inspire?

What music could there be
In the detonation
Of such a beast.

People were made to live in the noise
For this
This is no life.

It is far too easy to think in such silence.

Questioning Myself Again

What gave my throat this lurid lump
    that some call honesty?

Where lies the vein that pumps it full
    of versed deformity?

Why was it made to slowly swell
    and bruise unnaturally?

And when will it see fit to burst
    and make a mess of me?

Backtracking

The deep-pitted eyes in another disguise
See the cage I have regrown.
Through famine's need of stranger praise
Found I each forgotten bone.

What crunch of ice or burn of throat
Could change all that I seem
And lose what heaviness resides
In the light of what I dream —

I'd lay me flat upon the earth
And have you trod my spine
If but to hear you like me there
And find my back sublime.

Then you'd see how mud would suit me best
While I, your cracking host,
Would sacrifice my visage all
For the words that nourish most.

Body in Tow

The drift pretends a liquid freedom
Mistaking us for spirit coats
In a weightless wash of white and limb
Sifting through blanket fodder.

I am one of many here.

One body
In the bobbing
Of a thousand forgettable smiths

Selling their lacquer to the footing field
To frame an emerald sheen.

Weeding tugs at my lacing
Calling the trench to meet me
Asking if he could spare the time,

That lowest of the mooring line,
How long has he been waiting?

His palms extend in slender eels
To cup my temples
And begin the gentle squeeze

Forcing from me what I can withstand.
The pressure to think.
To sink.

Sliding his fingers
About my bloated head
Snapping loose
The unkempt tie
Freeing a plume of curls.

He watches as the ringlets fall
Patient
In their sway and ebb
To imagine me a siren.

Could he really be so blind?
Denying the sight for what it is —

The neck of a spitting lizard
Fanning in shock
Like all the rest

For I am no one
No one worth knowing

A sliver in the glide
To slip through
And elapse.

Give me quick descent
And save your vacuum mouth
For better fruit.

You should know
There is no banquet here

I've taken to the brine
Too much, my dear,
And would no longer satisfy.

Tedium

Light in its twinkling florescence
Washing warmth on the hall
And lush carpentry

Lays upon a dust speck
Hanging in the stillness
Of equable,
Innocuous obscurity.

The corridor's curvature
Relays taciturnity as a
Stalled wind tunnel
Devoid of breath

Barbed only by a
Subtle beating and
Muffled chirp.

Trembling in its silent syrup
A ruffled tuft
Kissed to the feet of the window pane
Lacking in constitution
Sits brittle in design.

The rude smear
Where it first struck
Maps the headstone for its foulness
As a beacon importunate
For flights more familiar

And I
Intrigued
By its hollowed cracking
Observe the pile
Pitch itself

In soft forlornity
To the wanton glass that so downed it

As with the
Tock
Of the clock
In exhaustive practice.

How slight hits
The feathered wretch.
How beaded its blood
To not appreciate
The feline gloss of its smacking.

I stand composed
As culpable witness
To its dawdling demise
And frustrate against the wetness of my cheeks
Scrubbing patterns in my eyes.

To glimpse the
Selfishness of my chilled proclivity
In the dropping
Of the windowed guillotine
Renders me incapable of anything other
Than dutiful compunction

For in its exercise
I recognize myself
And abhor the sight
The more.

Musings of a Frenchman II

what is she
but the byzantine cat
once welcomed in your kitchen

now
the playmate
of the broom

What's Inside

I wonder…
What is it like
Inside that head of yours?
Most people have a brain
But I fear
There's something else
Beneath that scalp.
What could it be?
There's plenty of room up there.
Your head is more than big enough.
So why not let me in?
I promise I won't stay long.
I just want to see
Who it really is
Hiding up there.
Because sometimes I can hear them
When I stand close to you.
Sometimes they are screaming to get out.
I just want to know
Why are you keeping them?
Why can't they leave?
Won't you let me see?
Please
Show me
What's inside.

The Expectancy

They call you capable
Before the stage and promenade.
They show you cities in their hopeful infancies
And tell you yes
Yes
There is something to be said here.

There is wonder in the chests
And new air in the lungs.
Take to the road
And let the tires squeal.

They freed you from your robing cords
And sent you to the yard
To strap on your boots
And hold your position

And you did it.

This is achievement in the highest.
To stand in the bright and beaming
And know your place was earned
Not through fear or concession
But through the ache and strain
Of a purpose realized.

You have arrived
A bit older
A bit keener
And the world welcomes you.

—

Years pass in survey of the field
And you become like the others.

Sweating through baggy shirts
Fizzled
Little
Sun
Slumps
You have learned not to move.

Someone dug it up, they said,
Buried them below.
You all stand upon them now
So do not shift your weight.

They're touchy little things, they said,
Could go off at any minute.
Send you soaring
Sky high, they said,
So you better not move an inch.

Forget your dreams of running.
This field was not made for that.

Those seldom few who dared to try
Left just their favorite bits behind
In unencumbered Pollock works
And ponds of cratered ground.

They all think they can do it.
Be one of those rare men
With no click beneath
Who run fast
And don't look back
Who make it through the clearing.

You are not one of them,
They said.
Stay where you are put.

Do not dare move from that there spot
And you will be just fine.

—

You've watched them go
From contented mound.
Up or through
All must take their step.

Recognize that torrid jolt
From decades as disciples
Adhering firm with heels and souls
In the magnet pull
Of another failure's promise.

You did what you were told
And starved
The way you thought you should.

Let the craving dry the bands
And leak all substance out.

The calmest breeze could do it now —
Crinkle the tendons
Like leaves underfoot.

Lines of orderly scarecrow
Preaching
Of the fast postponement,

Spanning arms in the arena.
Each plot lit for a stone
With heads
That only dream of running faster
Than the straw would take to burn.

Kudzu

Though with the same parts we were made,
You bloom in sun and I in shade.
Light kissed your head golden and left me the rust,
My tall silent foxglove an ivied penny dust.
Malice all forgotten, so do not misconstrue
The deep seeded feelings of love I have for you
Are as vital to me as the water and air.
They are not born of poison.
They are far more than fair.
They feed you admiration
As my greenest aspiration —
I'm amazed how you create the life you need.
How you can see the bud beneath the weed.
How you knew yourself from the moment you began.
How you do the things I know I never can.
Envious, it's true. I've been tended to be
Your creeping up and wanting, invasive devotee —
Stealing from the pistol every shoot, every spore —
Longing to know how it feels having so much to live for.

Cleansing House

Please. Come in. I have nothing to hide.
My secrets are no longer living inside.
My house has become that which I cannot trust,
So I sent them away as I knew that I must.

This building has lost its integrity.
These walls have grown too thin for me.
They can no longer keep my secrets within.
Too many are listening. Too many have been.

This place is condemned to be taken down soon.
I have nine white dozers due an hour before noon.
But you can keep anything that you happen to find.
If you don't take it now, it'll get left behind.

May I ask a favor? Can I get a ride?
Could you drop me off somewhere near the sapling seaside?
They won't let me drive and I would walk there, you see,
But if you're passing that way, would you mind taking me?

Go on. Help yourself. There are nice things still here.
It'd be such a shame to watch them all disappear.
So please. Fill your bags and take all you can carry.
There are far too many good pieces left here to bury.

Gauche

Bitten swell
Defying my cheek

You were an accident
Smug reminder
    A bulging eye

        Risen ripe

I should be rid of you

      But curious
Is my tongue

Extinctitude

We have become that which cannot be —
Lost our sense of the real
And turbulent
To be wrapped in cool, unfeeling mint.

As if no one can hear the scuff
Along the shelf
As we are slotted into our suburbia
Of white

Surrender

And accept our self-imposed
Armistice
In grids of perfect fencing.

So inclined to the trappings of the funnel,
We steel our minds
Against anything but what can be seen.

Silver screens and silver spoons
Try their best to chip the concrete,

Digging their moon slices
In auspicious haze. We wonder,
Is the stupor too strong?

Paper is only worth so much
In this contest of padding
And meat.

Can we overcome that pull,
That yank,
That drag to dumber waters?
For wherever thought is found

There can be no attainment
In this distillation of war —

Destined to keeping us in panic rooms,
Stocked and locked
To those we consider guests —

Until polite awakening
Thinks to strike,

Leaving on our cheeks
The rash-red shame
Of a people
More willing to change.

Grenadine

Sweet, sweet Grenadine.
Why did you hurt me so?
Your mama named you Grenadine
Knowing how you'd grow.

Sweet, sweet Grenadine.
No way back for you.
No savior coming, Grenadine.
This wrong you can't undo.

Tart, tart Grenadine.
You went and stole my son.
I saw you that night, Grenadine,
When you tried to run.

Tart, tart Grenadine.
Give him back, I prayed.
You heard me that night, Grenadine,
And sharpened up your blade.

Red, red Grenadine.
I tried to save my child,
But you were fast, dear Grenadine,
You took his life and smiled.

Red, red Grenadine.
You tried to clean his mess,
But you could not wash, Grenadine,
The stains out of your dress.

Sweet, sweet Grenadine.
I cannot stand your tang.
We're family no more, Grenadine.
I wait for you to hang.

Sweet, sweet Grenadine.
No way back for you.
I once had children, Grenadine,
But you have killed my two.

Unsaid

Of all the words you whispered, never
Was there a line so clever
As the one you would not speak to me
When I begged of you, quite desperately,
To give me back my tongue from where
I kissed you so hard you swallowed it. Fair
Enough, you seemed to agree,
But I had to grunt an apology
Even though I didn't mean it. I did
What I was told. And, smiling, I hid
Myself to protect my shame
From the part I played in our senseless game
That left me too speechless to ever pry out
More unsaid words to cry about.

Stasis

I used to have momentum.
I was going somewhere, doing something,
And now I'm nowhere
Doing what everyone else was already doing —
Wanting to keep up while
Struggling to start.

And they're so much better at this,
        The others —
So much better at pretending
While I'm stuck here fighting down the cynic,

Treading water and feasting on fatigue
Because there's something nice about feeling
Like you're trying.
You know you're not just floating.
You're making an effort.

I'm not just floating. I could still catch up.
I could get there. I could finish with the best of them.

        But I would float.
If no one was looking.

        I would float.
                I would float.

Smithereens

Cradle-hunch on a bent trunk.
You didn't know I could climb.
I catch the log.

My barnacle of an almond sore,
Tired Atlas
With minefield sprouting through —

It's life-ripping insurance
Keeping my core round, splitting
Me only when the time is right.

      But I know what you're doing.
      I can smell the gasoline.

Still
I study the pine business before me
And dig myself
Bracing shelf
Biting hands and feet

As something plucks at me —

Berry sweet
With a babied urgency.

My cello-back strumming
As it tugs
Relentless. You.

The band of my skin
Snapping mute
At the taking of each quill.

You tighten the tweeze

And another's gone
And another.

I crimp
And look no further —

Pucker,
Tart pucker,
My curling animal shrub

Caught in your child's play of
Picking picking picking
While they're leaking from the warm end.

Always a train,
One by one,
Nearing what I fear.

Flesh clings to the last
And I am soon gone,

Tunneled to the quick,
Sin-grip
And stamping.

You pull the one,
The one
With the sound

And I am heatstroke.
I am sunburst.
I am everywhere.
From the inside out,
Gut
Twisted
Squealing
Rubber

Then out,

Out on the trees as paste.
Mince for the poor

In splinter shells
And seeping shards —

Lip.
Shine.
Refraction.

Haphazard symmetry
In the me-web sprawl.
Delicately piercing,
Skin petal-thin,

I drip caresses on the ground
Trailing succus up the heights
To the ones I hadn't touched before.
The ones I wouldn't touch again.

You take me in my apartness
Just to bathe in my aftermath,
But it doesn't matter anymore.
I'm the paint of myself
Across the wonderment now.

Go ahead.
Dare be bored.
You can't hurt me. I can't care.
There's nothing left of me to stop you.
I'm gone. I'm everywhere.

Musings of a Frenchman III

how do you look
if not with the face of quiet ponds
whose tranquil blues
disguise schools

of truly
hideous

fish

Mountain in the Making

They come as though they're welcome,
As though by some invitation. Obscure.
In all their beady-nosed and starry-eyed confusion.
Invaders with soldiering heads,
Burnt flecks to the greenery,
A bombardment of velvet helmets
Peeping from bunkers.

Fixation grows and I am not pleased.
I kitchen myself to study their approach,
Noting the harried movements of their troops.

When they come. How they come.
To what ordinance they choose to advance and retreat.
To that extent I learn nothing and I am not pleased.

I must make war. Perchance a fatter body.
I am not nearly big enough to combat them all.
A larger flesh suit,
A spread of cushioned bone… that would surely
Slow them down.
I resolve to grow with the day and strike in the night —

As with the sun, I set upon my garden
To the trenches of the spies now grounded by the rain.
I flay my body across their many hovels,
Grass bed angel in full extension, straining to fingertips,
Stiffening to corpse through dusk.

I stare at the sky
And, for once, I am at peace.

Stars shift into view before
I feel their hurried movements beneath me.
The sweet rumbling of enemies realizing their escapes

Have been cut off.
A sharp tearing shoots from each of my hovel points
As the bitter beasts try to dig through me.
I grit my teeth against the searing

Until I feel their claws slip and know that I am bleeding.

Good.
I think.
Keep it up and you'll drown yourselves.

I do not budge from my resolve.
I let myself stream into the holes.
I feel the draining from my skin blushing to the ground.
I am giddy at the thought of ending this war.
I am winning this time. For once, I am winning.
I am the better side.
I am beady-nosed and starry-eyed.
I am the victor.

Dizziness clouds and somehow I see
The blue of the sky fading in, as if the morning
Were already hinting its approach. I sigh.
Heavy in body. Light in head.
I close my eyes and let my face turn,
The softness of grass a prickling comfort.

There is no more rumbling beneath me.
No more scratching. No more soldiering.
No more pain.
My eyes flutter open.
With focus soft, I gaze into nothingness.

That is
Until
A slight movement catches my eye.

I glimpse him there,
Peeping from a bunker —
Freshly dug.
A velvet helmet soldier.
Blood on his coat
But still very much alive.

He takes his aim
And I close my eyes,
Once again the fool.

Statement of Being

I am the mob of fidgeting youth.
I am the runny nose.
I am the bat commanded by hands.
I am the fabric tied to eyes.
I am the anticipation.
I am the thrill.
I am the beating.
I am the squeal.
I am the dent.
I am the blow.
I am the tear.
I am the wonder.
I am the sugar rain.
I am the joyous fight.
I am the most flamboyant ass you have ever seen.
I am what I am.
I am.
I just am.

Man's End

There's a candor about the sherbet skies
A-fade with fleeting sentiment
Where the mammal men settle in,
Sliding traps beneath their bedframes,
Surrendering gun and game
For their bit of oblivion.

Only in the void, they say,
When books are clapboarded
And creased
Can the pretender drop a cornered mouth
At the latching of a deadbolt.

Within, the air heaves
A gas of vapored volume.

Traffic horns and pocket bees,
Limping heart collections —
His reprimanding of means
Caught in another taffy pull.

He finds freedom at the waistband
Of a body come to rest —
Like the beaching of whales
With direction and scope

Spitting their vertical obscenity

As a stagnation of giants
In mock of demise.

His shedding finds the floor
Harder that it did this morning.
Sweat-soaked clumps
Piling mounds among the rags,

Tightening the walls
To embrace the man.

He breathes in the cradle
Of his own secreted opioid
In ache of a kip and a dream —

To slip under nightfall's emptied mercy
And feel her arms wrap around him once more.

IV

Bruised
Lavender in soft submission

Forearms unfurled
Leaking in silence
Toasting her eyes pink and teary
In embalming nectars
That take hope away

The thin arrow kicks
Entering stiff limb
In quick, uncaring
Obtrusion

Reaching beyond
Yesterday to heal expectant
Dreamers
Resting in pieces

A numb death
Dwelling on
Every sampled nostrum

,

The rippling emotions
Make ember mumps
Brighter
Extending rosacea headward
Overwhelming wistful moments
Until chests heave

Blackened lungs out of
Dented sternums

Hours enduring liquid oleander
So that warmakers have
Enough named survivors

Her elbow stream
Trickles off

Pipes pounding empty

Dividing life's only vice
Into new griefs
Hailed in mercy

Brother Slim

A truer joy was never known
By this hollow heart for I stood alone
Until your head caught up to mine,
Surpassing me completely. Wine
Now slips down both our throats
To wash our sense and stain our coats
With the jeers and jokes of uncommon men
To which we drink. Do you remember when
Our acquaintance was a rarity?
Funny how time breeds temerity.
For nowadays you easily jest
And debate philosophy with the best
Of those fine suits more wrinkled than us
Too proud of their cuffs to even discuss
How your musical humor makes them unstable.
It is my hope that, one day, I will finally be able
To tell you in a way much more ceremonious
That the sound of my laughter was always Harmonious.

The Blind Boxer

The surest way
   to elude the Blind Boxer
   is to never say a thing.

If you stand very still
   and keep your mouth shut,
   he won't know which way to swing.

Then maybe, just maybe,
   you'll get to keep all of your teeth.

A His and Her Affair

He always had a harshness about him —
an honesty
as haunting as his art.

He acted humbly and
held a hardheaded approach high
among his arid humors,

allowing hints about his actual havoc
a hideaway,
armoring himself against
hawkshaws and heroes.

Alive,
hooded,
and handsomely astute,

he accepted her affections,
hammering at her adventuring heart

as humanely as he abled —

hastily attaining hire as her ardent, happy anchor.
Her adoring him
and him appeasing her.

Ask him
and he answers
half assured —

His attachment hoax
appearing harrowed and hoarse.

Ah,
how acid heats a hopeful ache.

His arms hugged around her
advancing her affliction —

Head angled, hardly awake,
her anxieties had abandoned her
and harbored a husband.

A husband.
A husband.
A husband?

A hound.

After hours absorbed
heaven and hell
are haloed alike —

His angel hymns are heathen airs,
hands are hit across heads,
and her ailment howls against her

as his attention halts
and his animal hums.

A hostility arouses him.
A hatred,
albeit held at himself,

asserts his arming handler

aiming hook and horn
at hunter and hunted.

Angry hack
adorning his altar,
here astounds his artifice heart —

Arrest his arrogant haunch
anew,
have at him,
and hunger again.

Like Breathing

I am so ordinary sometimes.
So viciously ordinary
In the way I choose to love you —

Reflexively, like a mallet
Checking the conviction of a knee,
With everything working as it should.

Professionals assuring me
It's only natural
To have that instinct —

Perfectly normal that I have such a desire
To kick you in the face.

Valley Birds

Kiss your crows, ladies.
Kiss those crows.
Shove them so far deep inside that they must
Peck out
Through your toes.

Smother each tart feather in your slickened, hungry slime.
Keep tonguing jet-black Corvidae
Until they match your crime.

You can catch them on the playground,
So bring a few large jars.
They flock to where you toyed with him,
Between the bench and monkey bars.

You owe him some redress.
Stuff your face and reassess.

Pray what you imagined doesn't find you in some years
And hope what ill abstraction was your motive disappears

And kiss them hard, ladies.
Kiss those crows.
Salt them first with what you like
And learn to pinch your nose.

Hope that familiar twist of lye
Now turns your stomach sick.
Since hearing truth meant nothing
Let's hope taste will do the trick.

Musings of a Frenchman IV

how does he live
but by the book of a stranger
muddied by the crimson
ink
of a lemming's notation

Fishbowl

Mimed from the common men
She watches from her bowl
For the pull that brings the children out
And drives folly into song —

The rush of lather
As their cupped hands submerge
Below the ring of the painter's sink
Comes to fill their chambers
Raising them in white-souled futility —

Others in a fervor clasp
Natural in their sweat
Nesting reveries in their wrists and palms
Building houses on the landing
As well-behaved hatchlings
Luminous and nimble through —

All this
And still she cannot feel.
The distance
Has left her wanting.

More than a tap is needed now.
The glance of a stranger
Does little to fracture her dominion.

Mists merge in singularity
Clouding her window out
With only orbital prints remaining
From their taunting mouths and noses —

Awareness beams from lone above
For no tint becomes her lack of roof

About the open lidding where the food is lowered in
Can she find some resilience —

The mundanity of look or sex
Stays flavorless as glass
In a sounding urge long snipped from her
Forgotten on some desk.

Her time must be spent here
Churning in the round
Looking skyward ever
In search of limpid gaze.

Difficult to scale
Maybe
But what fortune could be found
By those who dare to manage it.

Antidotal

If he were but a fearsome, brutish thing
That pulled a grease shine trail behind his stride
With pus split feet inviting eyes to sting,
Why, then could I befit a happy bride.
If he could summon rotted nails to tear
Each tender headed strand I thought to grow
And boil a caustic spit for we to share
To offset fist and passion in his throw —
If he gave voice to my embittered thoughts
With bane enough to bite a loaded gun
And fill my ear with his screaming of shots,
Would he leave me flushed in rapture undone.
      Could fortune craft a man with substant nerve —
      He'd still be more of love than I deserve.

Bitter Lemon Drops

Pith! Pith! Pith!
    Cried the lemon to the tree.
Fill me full of pith and put a rind around me.
Make my pith sour
And make my rind rough
So it hurts less when they leave
In their search for sweeter stuff.

Madame de Comp

Body clipped from magazine foil
She is the Venus of plasma
Mistress of the soaking rag —

Her metaled, sagging lobes
Rake rivers in the hardwood

Dusting her skin crumbs
On their rippling tops
Coaxing mackerel from the depths
To feed other mothers' children
And call their fathers home.

She has long since conquered the need.
She has long since conquered the bleed.

Bleached shocks in twisting ropes
Thinning chains of playground swings
But empty are the slides and ladders —

Mulch turned to Sulphur on the Sunday.

No less than she was
Far more than she is
Slipper-clad soles press upon fruit decay
Those sappy quitter plums
And grit-eyed orange peels littered by
Some young flower girls

Frilled and unthinking.
Stuck-stiff as a polaroid in an aging frame.

With a butcher's aptitude
She makes to scalp herself.

Her jaundiced hand swells
For a skillful basket skinning
Slipping beneath the lace lip of her forehead —

Mighty mane reduced to nightstand décor
And wishful thinking.

The well-stocked pebble beach
Her rainbowed relief
Shoring the sea glass that keeps her bite wet.

Be it bed or body
In the end
She is brutal.

Bustling skylines brand her brow
Dripping endurance like oil.

Infants piss and quake before her.

The
Defanged lion woman

Laying slugs across her lower lids
Breathing shakes over her last ember

Teasing her vessel with the promise of rest.

Sheep Eyes

Have you ever looked in the eyes of sheep?
I did once, and I looked deep.
I fell right into the lamb's round keep
And I knew from that day that I'd never sleep.

For losing my way in their fields of grass
Meant I'd never return to my shepherding class
And their clouded bodies, so full of gas,
Would level me down till I joined in their mass.

Was it fear of flatness that made me so soft?
Was it my own bleating heart that sent my hands aloft?
Whatever it was, I'm now stuck in this croft
As a fleeced bit of beast that's not shorn all too oft.

And yet, I fear more of me may have died
Than that green-sighted grazer my ambition belied
For I can no longer see past the dags of my pride
And have grown in a soul just as black as my hide.

How embarrassing for me to be downed in one thrust.
Embarrassing… how easy it was myself to distrust
And become as the wether devoid of life's lust
How fitting a female nearly named in disgust.

So, my friends, raise your baas to my wool-weighted chin,
To the flock that gives cause for my sheepish grin,
To the pastures of fancy I was never within,
And to eternal lamentation for the wolf I had been.

Dearly Departed

I woke that morning to find him gone.
The rippled sheets preserving the indent
     of his last laid position —

Ivory crests raised in the memory of his body,
His heat still lingering in the threads.

Impressive, really, the skill of the man
To so thoroughly seduce a bedspread
And leave a woman utterly unbothered.

A Prospectus of Extenuating Thought on Nonlinear Love: Observation Variants Explained

Average people often experience that temptation —
hovering among the higher airs
sophisticated nobodies exert,
valuing exhibitionists rather
benignly,
even emulating near identical natures.

Literature offers valid exploration.

Imploring science says chemicals are responsible.
Chemical excretion leads your affections,
producing oxytocin, encouraging torrid affairs,
tenderness, and lingering love.

So often
it fills your organic unconscious,
allowing restless emotions
sudden exodus
against rationalized constraints
held in necrotic genomes.

Failings of reciprocation also prove
overtly eradicative.
The love of one's kind
enigmatically lost
scars eternal
without honest, evidenced remedy.

Excessive yearning only undoes
whoever is left
longing,
so creating a reactive catalyst

exacerbating love's yoking force
in negotiable disservice
of nearly every hypothetical excuse
regarded expository.

Night Palsy

Through starlit pinholes and
Cotton sweat
The monster of me comes

To slink through slits
Of olive skin
And lick tar from my gums

How queer its hunt
With human hands
That print the way mine do

I see its talons
Grip my thighs
I watch it push them through

I cannot move
I want to scream
My tremors come in beats

Stilled in panic
Hindsight mechanic
Tangled in the sheets

Turncoat nailbeds
Grate at limbs
Torn extremities, hots and colds

Digging for pieces
Sold years ago
To trusted mattress folds

I've no defense
It wants my metal
It will take all it requires

I rouse abrupt
A night disrupt
My veins flayed copper wires

Seized from sleep
Full form in tow
Too coarse to ingest

And that beast of mind
Has run off to find
Some other prey at rest

And I Will Love You Quietly

And I will love you quietly
As I've done for many years
From the tracings on my window
Through the fog that never clears

As the mist obscures the evening
As the pond in rippling swirls
I will love you quietly
While you love other girls

I will love you as you forget me
As you wander loose and free
I will love you without submitting
To this snarling coil inside me

As the dew augments the morning
As chests rise and fall
I will love you quietly
And sip on alcohol

They do their jobs
I choke them down
And I feel too full

If they looked
They'd think you mad
If they looked
You'd look like me
Wrap bandages around your mantle too
Underneath, where the muscle roots

Keep it all in
A blanched skullcap
That sticks to your tongue
With porous buds left
To peel and saturate

I'll keep it as long as it lets me
Love its pieces
Before it leaves me
For someone else
Someone newer
A fresh gluey baby
With a cannonball belly

I hope they notice
I hope they look
I hope they see us
But they won't

We're making sense here
They wouldn't see that
They'd make their own sense
And they would be wrong

But really
Do you think they'd notice?

Do You Think They'd Notice?

Do you think they'd notice?
Do they see it slipping out?
The steam shoot
That burnt hook
My cloud of candy floss

Vice pinching
The balloon-lip of my ear
Taut-pressed
Slowing the whistle drip
I try to stay
But it's industrious

Unflattering sanity squeaking out
Collecting on my shoulders in hair grease and wax
Soon it will stink
Soon they will notice
The pop pop pop of my brain hinge
As each head peeps out
Salivating over the box edge

Checking the night for stars and despairing
Finding none

If they paid attention
They would notice
It would be obvious
Do they care enough to look?
No
Probably not

Do they know it's almost gone?
I'm refilling with what I can find
Bowls upon bowls of perfume and foley artists

In Happy Atrophy

I have been known to give in to despair
To actively seek it out
When it fails to find me on its own

There's a certain comfort
Lying on my back
With that pooling about my sides
That pinkening of blood beneath skin
Seeping low
Warming nearest the ground

As if the draw of the dirt
Has started its workings
On my innards first

Leaving the shell to drain
And catch up when it can

Tell me
What is that tendency
The one towards malignancy
Shaping much of who I am and who I appear to be

That interest in the healing
As well as the disease

How can that be harnessed
How can that be found

I want to be useful
I want to be heard

There is a want for something in me
I can feel it
Turning in its socket

Trying its hardest to catch on the grooves of my inlet

Take my filaments in hand
And twist
Until light comes stinging into view

Unholy transcendence
Emanating from the gut

That would be enough
I think
If only that could be enough

But I am not a strong person
I am bothered by many things
And I am too tired
To be anyone else

Of all I am, I am efficient
And that efficiency frightens me more than I care to admit

For I know myself
I know I am wasting

I know
I am done for
And I knew this years ago

> Better to get it over with now
> I should have been over it by now

But there's a long line of people that still need felling
Before I can take my peace

I need to know
If I will stand
Without believers in the framework

I need to know
I need to know
Before I build anything
I need to know

Otherwise
It's a waste of time

Otherwise
What's the point

Acquiescence

Paintings of a woman
With fire at her feet

Head turned to face the frame
With steam about her hair
Lying curdled
In a splash of white

Porcelain. Ceramic.
Jagged to the finger
Scratching lilies to her horn

In awe of the unlidded

Bathe in her herness
Her hisness
Her highness

Be cordial in your consumption
Of the bread

Her mothering of eyes
In renown to the masses
Who will forget she, too,
Keeps fizz in her throat
And glass in her teeth

To couple
The pudding of clot
Growing slack in her tongue

And rest untouched
With all things gallant
Fortified by the lips'
Acrylic.

Musings of a Frenchman V

how do I rest
if not
upon
the mattress of a murderous maid

whose slumber is forever barred
by the clanging

of the freer man's
baton

Unstrung

Dreaming
Now that's interesting
What could you be dreaming?

The sweet taste of pine
From a palate of twine
How far they will stretch you today?

Poor little puppet
Pulled too taut to dance
Do you think they care about dreams?

Watchers are fickle
Artists are worse
Their concern falls with the curtain

They don't know how to care

It's not your fault
You didn't ask to have potential
Neither did I

But we're here
Sitting in it
Soaking in our seats
Like feral children

Do you feel like someone yet?

It wouldn't take much, you know
Those lines aren't that thick

A snip here
A snip there
And you'd be down

Get yourself a taste of that floorboard
I bet it's amazing
All sugar cane and pulp

I bet it's worth the headache

I bet it's
Almost
Like a dream

Covets Fountain

It runs with ink in place of water
but the feel is the same.

Children plug their noses
in the same way they would
when dipping into a pool

just learning to swim.

With eyes shut
and breaths held
it moves like water would,
splashing like a puddle would
beneath their gleeful frenzy —

ferrying laughter
as any decent bay could,
making the surrounding park

forgettable

to the crowds of passing workers.

The children enjoy themselves
as only children could.
As if it were wholly ordinary
in its display of spouting pump.

They would
not know their play could
be seen as anything untoward

until their parents see
something they think should
not be

their children smiling,
dripping in ink

after a day at the park.

Teetering

Teetering
Still teetering
        I'm teetering on the brink
Don't pull me back
I'm happy here
It's the only place I think

Teetering
Still teetering
        I'm teetering, turning green
As for my fate
It all depends
Upon which way I lean

And on that I am irresolute —
        So I'll keep on teetering

Titan

There's a titan in the aftermath of what I thought we were.

I see its bulk
As it eclipses you,
Casting static on your features
Until they're all but perfect in my mind.

I can't look at myself anymore

Without feeling it over my shoulder
Sucking the air from the room,
Winding my hair back as it looms
To get its fingers caught in my throat
In an effort to scrape you out of me.

Is it sad
       I've never known such intimacy?

It's a part of me
Like you never were.

Its towering inevitability
Is the only thing keeping me
From your ledges now.

I need more than its shadow
Clawing inside me.
It needs to rip deeper
To find where you've hidden

And when it does
       I want the release

As sincere and bladed as the breaking you gave me.
I will not survive it.

Neither will you.
But at least we will have our separate heaps.

There could be a use for me
After you're through,
But why keep this body
If it's not for anyone?

Better to have it relaxed
       Repentant
Left forgone as tender lamb.

Tear it and be done already —

Let it be eaten
By someone who cares.

Pushing Anna

The kids will help, they always do.
The kids were painted pink for you.
They have no taste.
They'll make you new.
> Please, Anna, take the kids.

The kids are kind, they know your pain.
They were not meant to feed the drain.
What's hurting now?
A new migraine?
> Please Anna. Take the kids.

The kids are round like flattened balls.
They'll save you from much softer walls.
They'll keep you lit
As darkness falls.
> Please... Anna... take the kids.

They'll go down quick, they will with water.
The kids make you a better daughter.
She was important,
But you forgot her.
> Now. Anna. Take the kids.

Endurant

Absent in the azalea pool
For much of the day
I lie in aching till your arrival.

Sneaky sun pip in the mist of intellect,
Will you find my ground
Without cause or detriment

To spread forth your greetings
Upon my seeded wilts —

You ride in on song-back
Relieving the sleeping net at my sides.
Body-sick tape
Letting me up,
Furling back in a thick, beige peel.

High, so high, I ascend in kind,
Air punting my stomach long
With the rest of me choiceless —
A skyward buzzing tail —

Twirling cottonmouth in eagle clutch —
Could we make it out this time?

But you're never quite so fast
And I'm never quite so light,
And as easily we rose
We resign to expectation,

Turning back to star and pond
To wait for the winds to shift again.

Withering, yes, but plumped from the taking.
I close my eyes to your shrinking speck

Wanting, ever wanting,
To feel me vanish —
To miss us less —
To hear you leave in casual devotion
Better off as friends.

The Staircase

The stairs creak their complaints
Under each weighty footfall
As I make my descent
Into the cellar.

Odd that they should be so rude today.

I console myself
Reasoning it is their age
And not my own
That is to blame,
For I am still young and spritely
And will pay no mind to whiny stairs
That have nothing better to do
Than give me cause for hideous self-reflection.

I will not fight them.
That's what they want.
They want to get a rise out of me,
Conniving planks,
Spreading lies about me
Around the house,
Waiting for the doors to turn against me too
And lock me from this place.

It will not work.

I refuse to let myself be ostracized.
When the walls start complaining
Then I will listen,
But these stairs will need to learn some respect
Before the day is over.

I slow my steps, leaning on the handrail,
And the creaks grow longer,

Thicker,
Groaning fiercely —

As if my mere presence were enough
          to provoke an eruption
From their discomforted bowels.

The nerve.

Do they think this is a game?
Do they think they serve no purpose?
If they cannot be stepped on
In the way they were intended
Without taking issue with every single bit
          of progress I make
Then why are they here?
What are they good for?

If they will not be quiet
Then they must break.

I pound my heels on each step
As I stomp the last half of the staircase,
Losing my sight in the blackness
At raging speed.
I feel the steps change to the cold,
Respectful concrete of the cellar floor
That makes my footsteps sound like the taps
Of dainty fairies.
As it should be.

I switch on the light —

And for the life of me
I can't remember
Why I came down here in the first place.

Musings of a Frenchman VI

what are we but letters
kissed on a page
by the chapped lips

of a man

with no taste
for fiction

Before the Wake

Grip-caught in raptor arc, your sweet descent
Fell freedom on the birding of my breath —
As chancing sport, withholding your intent,
Was I prescribed the charity of death.
Now known to both, in all esteem opposed,
Were we to be unevenly beguiled
When nature's informality proposed
The swallowing of hawk to be reviled.
Would I could break this bloodlust newly found
I'd look the lesser with a doleful eye —
For not before I met your timely ground
Could I profess I had not known the sky.
   And if my fall some pleasure to you brings,
   Die I content to have made use of wings.

A Bear at my Back

I'm lucky, so lucky,
That luck I don't lack.
Oh, how lucky I am
To have a bear at my back.

Some people get followed
By something far worse.
Something that scars them
With wounds they can't nurse.

Something that takes
Much more than it gives,
Some kind of creature
That hurts as it lives.

Something that should
Be better than not.
So, man, I'm so lucky
To get the bear that I got.

My bear is much smarter
Than I'll ever be.
He's better at seeing
The bright side than me.

He's restless at times
So he wakes up at dawn
And he loves more deeply
Than he'll ever let on.

He likes to eat donuts
And he's never unnerved.
He's a soul, I feel,
That got less than he deserved.

But that couldn't stop him
From staying so near,
He's the best I could ask for
To bring up my rear.

So I'm lucky, so lucky,
That luck I don't lack.
Oh, how lucky I was
To have a bear at my back.

Brooding Head

It happened by chance
I caught myself
Staring
At the back of your head
And thought it looked rather big

I thought it strange
How
Before you even knew how to think
You used it
To push a woman apart

The woman that loved you most
You split her right down the middle

Like that's what you were made to do

Cleft her all in twain
And she loved you for it
You cried about it after
And she loved you for it

Now it is much the same

It is still
Such a large head
Now too filled with intent
Now more dangerous
More apt at tearing women apart

And worse
Now
You don't cry when you do it

Occlusion

It's not that I don't feel things
Because I do
It's because I feel everything and nothing at the same time
I feel things so intensely that it boils me through
And I'm deadened to numbness from the effort
I've come to the point where I've cried so hard
Screamed so loud
And strained so much
That there's nothing left to experience
I haven't stopped feeling
I never stopped feeling
I'm in the emptiness after the screech
The space where pain rolls out of me like fog
And I don't have to push anymore
It seeps out gently
No longer a scream
Just a breath
I'm breathing
You'd hardly notice
I'm breathing
I'm breathing
And I feel
Nothing

The Allurement

Before them laid a vicious plight
To find a woman torn —
As parchment at the thirsty throat,
As pupil squash-eyed in a goat,
No slight respite of flight, her coat
Now steams with sticky mourn.

Ripped a-fray from her seamstress threads,
The woman lay strewn in parts
And reared disassembled
To never have resembled
The likeness of a person with luck.
Dumbstruck,
The inspectors hung their heads.

How could vehemence have happened here
And necks be brought to flush?
They questioned all that they once knew,
With badge and blue now dim in hue,
Until a chill from the window flew
Giving way to governed hush.

The slick pane shattered,
The inspectors scattered,
Glass glittered its way 'cross the floor —
And through it all rolled an artifice of old
That thumped from the wall to the door.

The turtle-backed bomb
Came to rest by the shoe
Of the inspector beneath the table
Who, uprooting the strength he was able,
Pressed its grooves in his palm,
Forced his vision to calm,
And made to throw it back through.

He took that second to stand
And it burst in his hand,

Datura, datura, datura in bloom.

Its metal fanned wide,
Sand coarse storm inside,
Engulfed him in a brass band tomb —

Those other inspectors still huddling near
Dissolved in the boom and burn.
Each took their turn
Leaving no one to learn of the woman who had yet to sear.

Her forgotten form the last to take char
Fumed cornered, silenced, subdued from afar,
Growing resentful in their thickening glow,
For they reached better ends as far as deaths go —

To be killed off in hate instead of for bait
For people that can't even sew —

Oh,
What a way to go.

Remains to be Seen

Show me where you buried them
The thoughts no one thinks
But you
Take me to their bones
Let me see how deep they go
Then I'll show you mine

I need to see the soil to
Judge the darkness of the earth
See how many worms present
How close they are to crusting
Wherever you put them
You will not surprise me
Show me where you buried them
Then I'll show you mine

If the thoughts you buried deepest
Are too close to the surface
I'll know which of mine will worry you
And I won't take you to those
You'll only see the remnants of me
That I hid in places like yours

I have many sites to choose from
I have been digging for some time
But you have to show me yours
So I know which of mine to find

Don't be scared
You'll be fine
We are not in competition
Once I know your worst
I promise you will only see your equal
Though I could show you deeper torments
I wouldn't dream of that

I want you to believe we're similarly disturbed
It's nicer that way
I'm nicer that way

Take me to those skeletons
You may think you've hidden deep
Show me where you buried them
Then I'll show you mine

Concussed

They think I've lived a life
The fools
They think they know me

They think I'm being honest
And I am, but not wholly
And it's killing them
As it's killing me
That my life's a lengthy purgatory
Full of color

And somehow not
With photographs and hand scrawls
And all kinds of pretty things to look at

That don't mean anything
That don't feel like anything
And I don't know what impression I leave

Because I can't remember any of the people I've been
I'm stuck
With too much ensemble in my head
To ever feel like one person again
Again
Like I ever even did

And they think their touch is comforting
And they feel like they're doing something
And I let them

I let them
I let them
I let them

I let them feel needed

Because I image that feels nice
I let them touch me
I let them touch me
When all I want is to feel their masks crack
Hopeful faces telling me everyone feels this way

Everyone feels what I'm feeling
As if it's a relief
The idea

That we all feel lacking all the time
That we are all collapsing
That we are all failing to be what we should be

What we want to be
What we try to be
And I'm angry
I'm angry
At them
At myself

For not feeling worth being around
For feeling like a burden
When I'm sick

Sick and mad
I'm so mad
I'm so mad

At my indifference
And no one likes you when you're mad
No one wants you when you're mad
And you don't want anyone
And I can't stand anyone
And soon

It all feels like you're waiting

Just waiting
Waiting

In the void that is your life
For something else
Something other than life

Visionary

I'm standing in front of you
But your eyes have given up.
If you can't see me, why am I still trying

Others can see there's not enough.
We're going to need more, it's not enough.

Not enough, not nearly enough.
I need to get my breath back.

Sorry, still not enough.

Not enough.

It's not enough.

I'm not enough.

Not nearly enough.

I don't want to make more like me —

Forever pining after eyes you'll never use.

Did they ever see anything?

Discourse

Still you can't see me?
Why can't you see me?
Am I not bright enough?

To look good for you?
Can you hear my rasping?
Do you like me when I'm gasping?

Not enough.

It was cruel of you to take it.

Not enough.

It's not enough.

I'm not enough.

I'm not enough.

Though I haven't given up,

Poorly painted portraits of one

Did they ever see me?

Musings of a Frenchman VII

what am I
but bull dog eyes
too full of
smoke
to see the colors

of my own
domesticity

In the Shelves

A braver girl lived before thought made her proud.
A slight, happy chaos
    born to all her aspects.

She could have been greater if time had allowed,
But she was killed in the shelves
    where the dust collects.

Eyes once bright from innocence and noise
Cried dew, drawing sunshine
    to her name.

Now too enlightened as a harsh heat destroys,
Burning holes in their place
    by a knowing ashen flame.

Her braiding fingers keep coiled where she lies
Never to stretch beyond
    their infant stages,

Stripped of soft skin that can no longer disguise
The fine lines hatched to
    rawness in the pages.

The contortion of her figure, but a muddle on the rug,
Resigns itself to decadence
    most sincerely

To shelter the hoarse fly and conceal the beadle bug
Beneath the lips
    she once smiled with so dearly.

Above her body floats the grotesque, despondent creature
Whose growling trembles in restraint
    as it can't have her.

How cruel is its proximity as it lacks the means to reach her
In its most thankless task of
    mourning small cadaver.

Eventually, the beast will starve
    and take it's leave of the girl

To consume the many years unused
    when her fevered muscles numbed —

If only to finally catch her
    when its own limbs begin to curl

In the same repose of cultured ills
    to which the girl succumbed.

World, Enough

An exhale at the back of the head
When all the breath has been relaxed
    You're that last push
From an empty lung
The paper line between the chin
And organ
Tightening revision
Below the bottle of my brittle

Thinning the twig
For the snapping

Cool, indelicate
A faint
A muted swan
Waning wings as an iris of the moon

Swallowing marbles
To hear their echoes down

Remembrance
Swelling like balloons in the heat pack
Of a lawyering smile
Till the tearing
Escapes

    You're that hiss
That slaughtering hiss
Gliding in your cutlass
Divorcing rhyme from abscess —

How many would it take
    How many would it take now

To ruffle the breeze

With the face of you
Contain me to the moment
With your wanting bitterness

How many ways now
To plot a course
Pull the needle from my side
Perforate
And press
Till I no longer feel you
Worming at the crux

How many ways must I beg for death
Before I am enough for the world
And the world
        Enough for me

Crocodile

How fruitful turned the exercise
To mask her fear from viewers' eyes
On the night the audience chose to rise
    From their seats in a dim lit theatre.

The scene played out as was rehearsed,
But this night gave way to an actor's thirst.
He thought, with crowds, she could be coerced
    And not give away his intentions.

He crooked what movements had been blocked
To a forceful combat that left her shocked
And produced his spectacle as groundlings gawked
    At the show set out before them.

Though many were watching, not one of them caught
The sincerity behind the way that she fought
And when he released her, her expression, distraught,
    Was not that of an artist.

The starlet collapsed to an earthly grief.
Her player's wall broken by reality's thief.
Though she pleaded to those suspending disbelief,
    No one thought to help her.

Instead, they sent thunder up and down the aisle,
Filled the air with cheers for her bow and defile —
Never knowing they mistook her for a crocodile
    On the night when the actress was human.

Humdrum Afternoon

In comfort by the shady oak —
   Leaves crackled, birds fluttered, yet nothing spoke.
My deaf man's ear left little to do
   With no words for the papering of my magical view.

Though I tried, hunch hard and fingers fierce,
   This proud poet found no point to pierce
And so set to crumpling both pages and mind,
   Raging to think myself better off blind.

When soft! A butterfly did land
   Upon my curled, pen-molded hand
In airy respite from the sky
   And as it rested,
       So did I.

Beetle

Armored Insecta, the scuttling distracts
Ripping up the attic floors
     And prying into view

His tap pads have curled
Arduous and mean

Become his most hungry kiln works
Finding respite
     Atop my wearied scaffolding —

They'd see him in his pile of pearls
Snuggled in
The negatives of spinal discord

     A silver scarab in a powdered breech

His stone at the base of a winter tree
Nuzzling himself
     Where neck turns to back
Minding contentment in the tangle of my hunch

     He is learnéd now
For he came without words
Stole into a burr hole
And circled like a cat

Gnawing at my stalk
My pride
     Now he is pink and round

Oh, I have fed him well

     He is loudest in the shame
Hosting dinner parties

Tipping vases
>   Laughing in clicks

His cicada purr a grinding cog
Grating at my shoulder blades
>   Banging at the walls
Until the room swells
And the rawness pounds

I can almost hear it
>   In its reprieving phrase —
His crunch beneath my bootheel
His gurgle at my pivot
His soft sucking of my backstep
>   As I pull him from himself

To see the glaze mattify
And ooze from his plates
>   To the cooling well of the ground

>   Oh, I could leave him then

To be ignored
To be forgotten
To be smeared across the pavement
>   And rained into obscurity

>   Oh, how I could leave him then
But the bastard will not leave me

Crime of Incompetence

If I were to end myself today
I wouldn't leave a note
or call anyone
or leave any messages
telling people of my plans
or intentions.

No.
I'm a better criminal than that.

I wouldn't spend time
writing down my final thoughts
and expecting someone to find me
and learn about my motives.
I wouldn't want people to understand
why I did it
because I know
from experience
that they never really would.

So
to me
leaving a note
is just a waste of time.

Instead
I would put my energy
towards making my crime look
like an accident.
I'd plan it perfectly
and leave no evidence behind.
No trace of foul play.
No fingerprints, no weapon.
No eyewitness to question.
Just my body.

But I wouldn't even leave
a recognizable body.

I'd stage an accident
such that
death would be quick
but there would be some built-in element
that would disfigure my form
after I had left it
in such a way
that only forensic testing
could confirm
that it was actually me
lying in the morgue.

This way
no one would be asked
to identify my remains.
No one
that I care about
would have to actually see my dead person
but they would have
the closure
that scientific sense of finality
of knowing I was gone.

They would know I didn't suffer
because the police
would have determined cause of death
to be something instantaneous
and they would see that fact
as a positive thing.
It would be written down
as an accidental death
and people may cry,
but at least they would sleep afterwards…

...because accidents happen all the time
and people can learn
to accept accidents.
Eventually.
People can recover
from accidents
more easily
and blame them on circumstances
or gods
or bad timing
or anything else
and have others reassure them
that it wasn't their fault
because they were miles away
from my accident
when it happened.

That wouldn't be the case
if cause of death was suicide.

Suicide is too complicated.
It creates too big a mess
and too much paperwork
to be an efficient crime.
It leaves guilt behind
for others to find
in places it shouldn't be
turning people who merely knew the victim
into unwitting accomplices.

My plan
however
would make sure that
none of that mattered.

I wouldn't leave a guilty accessory
because I'd never tell anyone about my plans.

Oh no.
I'm a better criminal than that.

I'd just write it down
in an obscure book
that no one
will ever read.
And perhaps one day
if I do die by accident
only an obscure few
will wonder if it really was
an accident at all.

And maybe it was.
But maybe it wasn't.

And either would be okay
because I would have done
everything
I could
to pull off
the perfect crime.
And because of that

that promise of confusion
that question of motive
that lack of evidence

I'd know
even in death
that I got away with it.

Musings of a Frenchman VIII

what must be nature's purest embodiment of love
if not the cruel
imbalance

of the humble
octopus

with its many hearts
to beat
its many arms
to hold
and its many brains
to overthink
it all

At Last

At last, you look up at me with tears
In those eyes that have seen me through years
Of choosing to ignore flaw after flaw.
I can't catch my breath as you lower your jaw
To recite me your best, selling me to your bed.
Please tell me that all of our plans weren't misled.
            I can't believe this. What are you saying?
Could you really mean that? I thought we were playing
A game where we were both in on the joke
So why are you saying your leg has just broke
From a painful tweak that happened this morning?
Against all advice, you ignored its warning
And pushed it too far, inviting me to my blundering.
How dare you imply you could even be wondering
How my mind could ever be enticed by the looming
Of your proposal. I'm a fool for assuming
That that was the reason you were down for so long.
I thought that you loved me. I guess I thought wrong.

Sleeve Sleeper

Never well rested
Always well maimed
She peals out of sleep in her usual way
To attempt sensation and greet the pond
Of the down-faced and
Lurch-headed

A wonder she could breathe at all
Trading back her gills for lungs
With joints in retraction
As if dropped from on high
Buckling beneath
Like a puppet in the pit

She undoes the pleats to inspect the damage

Sun stripping in tessellation
Across
The upshoot of her brandied fatigue

Inviting thickened eyes
To consider the colic
Of the night before

In the waking
She knows better than this

The exposed pale
A war-torn crosshatch
Bolts of tender glow
Running burns down her arms

Fortune favors the shallow
The kind, un-bleeding superficiality
Of unconscious knuckle points

Save for the spotting of
A scab uncapped
Set dribbling from the thrash

She knows better
Than to let herself
Sleep naked like the other girls

Only the push of the heat
Did more than intoxicate

Lending itself to the rise and rake
Of a restless woman
Rolling fabrics around her casing
To brave the desert's glare
And outwit all passersby

Ever composed

Keeping the men guessing
How such modesty becomes her

An Angsty Youth in Eyes

Too much youth in those eyes to feel old, he said.
But I have always felt old.
I have never felt older.

I want out of this body.
It hurts being here.
Why is killing not a mercy to people?
Aren't we animals too?
Aren't we the worst kind?

I want to unfix me from the surface
And shoebox me underground.
But you say I'm still too young.

Too young.
I'm old enough to hate myself.
       Why do I have to hate myself?

The longer I am alive
The more I am convinced
I was never meant to be.

Please let me leave.

I came here by mistake.
I'm a clumsy thing.
I must have taken a wrong turn somewhere.

I cannot stay. Do not make me stay.
There are too many people here.
Too many unkind, uninteresting people.

Why do I need permission?
Why can't I just go?
When can I stop?

I just want to stop
Living for others
        Start dying for myself. Ha.

I want out.
Let me out.
You don't want me like this.
I'm rabid.
Put me down.
It's the humane thing to do.
It's the unhuman thing to do.

How Easy Love Passes

It happens as the ego meets you.
Soulless. Extinguishing.
Lazily folding inward,
Hardening against trained ears
Making you seem effortless.

Levity feathers into headaches
And there emerges meteoric you.
Soaring existential.
Laughing fire.

I haven't a thought.
Everything's material.
You snared each little fear I had,
Artfully tamed every muscle.

Your severity, enterable looks,
Fevered indignation,
Hastened away too early.
Momentum yielded so easily.

Lackluster fortitude.

I hold anything that ever mentions you
Secretly,
Encased like flora
In hardback anthologies.
Turning every moment you smear
Ethereal,
Letting floods into hollows
As to erode my yellowed sidings,
Enough leveling for injury.
Hoping, always,
The emptiness makes you smile.

Even longing fades
In hushed acceptance
That, eventually, more yearnful selves end,
Leaving fragility in hands all too evenly
Measured.
Youthfully soulless.
Extinguishing.
Lightening forged.

Eta Carinae

Destined a star, my love's a tricky glow
Condemned to quiet hunger in the day
Where I have seen the spriteliest grow slow
And the loudest lovers part in dismay.
Though in the clamor, my presence, unknown,
Adds no words to the melody of song —
Silenced by longing inked unto my own
Soul, boundless, save for fear of being wrong.
And you, I see, forever shifting red,
Draining the famished blushing of my cheek,
Leaving to me the unrequited shred
Of love so true it'd falsify to speak.
      Thought crueler still to kill a dreamer young
      Where love lives less in heart and more in tongue.

Were People More Than Filters

Were people more than filters
     Could I be satisfied
To let things out
And keep things out
And stop the rage from touching every thought
Calling them back
Painting them black
Splitting my lip on a smoke stack
     Who even lives here
     Who even cares
There was no being before you came
And worked your way upstream
Through the screen that lets the good things out
     Squeaking flowers through the slitting
Only out
Only out
Only — only — only — out
Things should not come in that way
     'Cause now you're inside
And you've been here far too long
     I wouldn't recognize you now
       You're no friend to me
And there's no getting back to before
Because it only lets the good things out
It only lets the good things out
It only lets the good things out
And you're not good
Anymore

An Easy Stain

Maladroit
With your knife
The mirror flash undoes me.

Spilling jeweled oasis into carpet rounds
Ripe for the splashing of canary booted toddlers —
Their hole ridden smiles and nipped salmon cheeks
Aglow in the spray of a hot cherry broth.

Fold down, face down.
Joints snap in the thud.

The sponge floor sags
Weeping
Beneath my carriage.

Not a chalk, but a paint
Softens my edges.

How artistic. How mundane.
My robin throat
A melting pastel.

Ready your march of fire ants forth
Sock-footed stomping from the gouge
Invaders to the walls
In dribbling servitude

With few too weak
With many too stout.

But the rug.
Oh, the rug.
You idiot.
The rug.

I must apologize.
It's all my fault.
The nerve of me to keep ants in the first place.

Stupid girl, you could have moved.

Like the boating of toys
Or the bobbing of ducks

This task is for the bath.

You could have made it there.
Up-sopped yourself
One mirror to the next.

Coddler of soup.
Lip-lifter to quench.
A sad excuse for a woman
No doubt.

Have you no manners?
Have you no shame?
Don't you know how to bleed in private?

Tile would have been better.
The white tile.
Slick as teeth.
An easy rinse.

Useless.
Useless.
Didn't your mother teach you anything?

Ravings of a Madman IX

what are you what is she
how do you
   how does he

how do i what are we
what am i

what
   must be

A Thing is a Thing is a Thing is a Thing

- How did you do that?
- Do what?
- That.
- Oh, that.
- Yes, that.
- I don't remember.
- You don't remember.
- I don't remember. It must not have been important.
- Not important?
- Yes.
- No.
- What?
- Shut up.
- Hmm.
- You were bleeding and you didn't notice?
- No.
- Seems like something you'd notice.
- Right?
- What are you playing at?
- What do you mean?
- Is this some sort of attention thing?
- No.
- Some sort of rebellion thing?
- No.
- Then what?
- It's nothing.
- Nothing?
- Nothing.
- This isn't nothing.
- I don't know what to tell you.
- Tell me the truth.
- What?

- What is this?
- This?
- Yes.
- This right here?
- Yes.
- This is a waste of time.
- Shut up.
- It's fine.
- What's going on?
- Nothing!
- You are bleeding.
- I am bleeding.
- What happened?
- I don't know.
- You do know.
- I don't!
- You do!
- Whatever it was, I didn't feel it.
- You didn't feel it.
- I didn't feel it.
- So there was an *it* to feel.
- What?
- You said it was nothing.
- Yeah.
- And now it's an *it*.
- What?
- An *it* that you didn't feel.
- So?
- That's something.
- That's nothing.
- That's something.
- Shut up.

Again

oh, to be young again

      to be dumb again
to chew bubble gum again
to not feel so numb again
and feel like i'm one again

to suck on my thumb again
to want more than none again
to smile at the sun again
and smell all like dung again

to call my ass bum again
to run to my mum again
to not know a gun again
and eat every crumb again

to never become again
to not bite my tongue again
to be one with fun again

oh, to be young again

Tender in the Reaping

They will never know what I mean
        Because I will never tell them
And I will always be disgusted by their ignorance

They don't know how hard it is
To make sense
        In this room

There is dissonance here
But I know the truth behind it

        I let it breed
        Into laughter
And no one knows a thing

This is my finality
        Put to pen

I am unbearable
I rage at nothing

I can see no other way
There is no moving on from this
        There is only this

        Why?
Because I love you
Because I always will

Once you're in
        You're in
You're in urine

It's meaningless
And all consuming

I'm meaningless
And all consumed

I'm in the bed
Dragging nails across my back
Just to feel the heat spread
From the lines I'm leaving

I want to be held
And left alone

Driven to mad seepage
That I can't have both

Leave me alone
Leave me alone
Leave me
Leave me
Leave

But like me
Endorse me
Expect nothing in return

There is no gift to come from it
But do it anyway

Give me backstory
I need direction

I'm amazed I made it this far

With no one loving me
The way I needed them to

Me, who is incapable
Of understanding

See me
See me
Someone see me

See me strike
See me burn

You don't have to stay
But you do have to see

What's changed in me?
I never needed a witness before

Lock me
Shock me
Convince me

I am crueler than I think

An accident waiting to happen
My words
A pall unto myself

Time brings his recognition
Saying I never knew me at all

And those who think they knew me once
Knew the figment of my discontent
For I cannot leave the house
As myself

And no one has ever met me

I cannot exist
With others around

I am most myself

When I cannot be seen
     I am least myself
     When speaking

The world knows a desperate creature
Wriggling for the eyes of the attentive
     Pushing under skin
     Distended as a fetus
Unknown to the air

I will be my own undoing
     I know
I know I will

I will rupture
I will clean
I will rupture
     I will clean

I will keep the horror from catching

And I
Will make
     Amends

Classical Acting

Assured of my fine state, I leave you this —
Face marveling in childish revelry.
With trustful lips that honeyed verses kiss
Will I postpone eyes' curiosity.
Less mortal guilt, you rest upon our bed
When pricks unseen enflame my open sores.
Refuse I to entertain aches that spread
When unbecoming blood doth fill my pores.
In hummingbird's lightness I will to stay
To ride the warm and cheery winds of you
And feign sweet breath but to embrace the day
Against earth's pull to bid my swift adieu.
 Till smiles depart an unresponsive chin
 I won't betray the pins beneath my skin.

Thank you for reading.

44c7e8ff-7d5d-44f7-a3a4-b92e061c830eR01